Make IT Now —
Bake IT Later! #5

More "Make - aheads" —
All easy —
   and fun To prepare !

Grosset & Dunlap, Inc.
New York, NY 10010

Notes

This book is dedicated
to
Courtenay Pickett —

a brave little girl —

a valiant struggle.

And all along the way she
brightened the days for
others —

Notes

Table of Contents

Notes

No Work Chicken

So good — and it's best when prepared the day before!

Chicken breasts for 4
½ cup honey
½ cup Dijon style wet mustard
1 Tablespoon curry powder
2 Tablespoons soy sauce

Place chicken snugly, skin side down, in flat baking dish in one layer
Make marinade by mixing together the honey, mustard, curry powder and soy sauce. Pour over chicken and refrigerate 6 hours or overnight.
When ready, turn chicken, cover dish with foil and bake at 350° for one hour. Remove foil — baste well — and continue baking, uncovered, for 15 more minutes.

When serving, spoon sauce over chicken.

Serves 4 —

1

Notes

Cheesy Zucchini Bake

It's Tasty, easy, lo-cal, and inexpensive!
What more can you ask?

1 lb. lean ground beef
½ yellow onion, chopped
½ Teaspoon garlic powder
1 lb. fresh zucchini
6 oz. (generous) longhorn cheese, freshly grated
1 can (10¾ oz.) mushroom soup, undiluted

Brown meat with onion and garlic powder. Drain off any excess grease.

Wash zucchini and cut off Tips. Do not peel. Cut in ¼" slices. Cook for no more Than 5 minutes in small amount of boiling water. Drain.

Grease a 1½ qt. baking dish and put in a layer of half The meat — Then half the zucchini — Then half The cheese. Repeat layers.

Mix soup with ¼ cup water and pour over Top.

Refrigerate. When ready, bake at 350° for 40 minutes, uncovered.

(I Tried it with regular cheddar. Good, but not nearly as good as with longhorn!)

Serves 4 — maybe!

2

Notes

Dinner for One, please, James!

Put one fairly thick lamb chop (shoulder chop is fine) in small flat baking dish or small foil pie pan.

Spread chop with chutney.

Bake, uncovered, at 350° for about 40 minutes.

And, a little fancier?

1 meaty chicken breast
   red wine (about ⅓ cup)
½ can (10¾ oz. can) cream of chicken soup
1 sandwich slice of Swiss cheese, cut in slivers
¼ pkg. (3 oz. pkg.) smoked sliced beef, cut in slivers

In the morning (or night before) put chicken in baking dish as above, skin side down. Pour on wine and refrigerate.

When ready, turn chicken and spread undiluted soup over it.

Bake, uncovered, at 350° for one hour.

Spread beef over chicken and top with cheese. Spoon sauce over all well. Bake 15 minutes more.

3

Notes

Quiche

Served often by a NYC bachelor who
is a great cook.

1 pie shell (9") uncooked
1/2 lb. Swiss cheese, finely diced
1/2 lb. ham, finely cubed
5 whole eggs
1 cup Half and Half
1/4 Teaspoon salt
   several dashes nutmeg

Fill shell a little more than half full
   with alternating layers of cheese
   and ham. Refrigerate.
Beat together the eggs, cream, and salt.
   Refrigerate separately.
When ready, stir egg mixture with a
   fork and pour over pie. Sprinkle
   with nutmeg.
Bake at 400° for 15 minutes Turn oven
   to 325° for 30 minutes. Cool 10
   minutes and serve promptly.
   Follow recipe exactly — or it may
   get soggy if it stands too long
   out of the oven.
This is really delicious, and actually
   it makes more than enough for
   9" pie shell.

Serves 4 —

4

Notes

Covina Crab

A popular party dish!

5 pkgs. (6oz. each) frozen crabmeat, thawed
   Can use same amount canned or fresh -
12 hardboiled eggs, chopped
  6 slices white bread
  2 cups Half and Half
  2 cups real mayonnaise
  2 Teaspoons lemon juice
  2 Tablespoons grated yellow onion
  1 Tablespoon dried parsley flakes
  1 can (4oz.) pimientos, drained and chopped
  1 can (8oz.) mushrooms, drained
     salt and pepper To Taste
     Cornflakes, crushed

Trim crusts from bread and cube bread.
Combine all but Cornflakes and mix gently.
Place in large, greased casserole and
     refrigerate.
When ready, sprinkle Cornflakes all over
     The Top and bake for 1 hour at 300°,
     uncovered.

Serves 8 amply —

Notes

Layers

Meat, potato, and vegetables all in one!

1 lb. lean ground beef
3 carrots, peeled and sliced
3 stalks celery, sliced
1 large baking potato, peeled and sliced
1 medium yellow onion, peeled and sliced
1 small green pepper- remove seeds and
    white membrane. Chop the pepper.
1 can (4 oz.) mushrooms, drained
    salt and pepper to taste
1 teaspoon each dried basil and parsley
1/4 teaspoon dried tarragon
1 can (10 1/2 oz.) tomato soup, undiluted

Break up meat into bottom of 2 qt.
    baking dish.
Put carrots on top of meat, then celery,
    then potato slices, onion, green
    pepper and lastly, the mushrooms.
Add seasonings over all, and cover
    with tomato soup.
Refrigerate, covered.
When ready, place in 350° oven for
    2 hours, covered.

Good with green salad and hot
    french bread!

Serves 4 (If you want more, use 2
    large potatoes.)

6

Notes

Lamb Moussaka

An unusual Treat for 10!

3 lbs boneless lean lamb, cut for stew
1 cup flour
4 Tablespoons salad oil
1 medium yellow onion, chopped
2 cloves garlic, minced
1/2 cup red wine
1 can (16 oz.) whole Tomatoes, undrained
1 1/2 Teaspoons salt, 1 Teaspoon dried rose-
    mary, 2 Teaspoons dried parsley flakes
2 small eggplants, peeled and cut in 1 1/4" cubes
1/2 lb fresh mushrooms, sliced

Shake lamb, a few pieces at a Time, in
    flour in paper bag.
Heat oil in large frying pan and brown
    meat well. Put meat in greased 5 or
    6 QT. casserole.
Slowly cook onions and garlic in pan
    drippings until glossy. Add a bit
    more oil if necessary. Stir To pick
    up all particles. Add to casserole.
Pour wine into pan and simmer a minute
    or so.
Add Tomatoes with juice (breaking up
    whole Tomatoes) and add seasonings.
    Cook, stirring often, for 5 minutes.
    Pour over lamb and refrigerate,
    covered.

(cont'd)

7

Notes

Lamb Moussaka (cont'd)

Peel and cut eggplants and put
in refrigerator in plastic bag.
Slice mushrooms and do likewise.

When ready to bake, add eggplants
and mushrooms to casserole,
Toss gently, and bake at
350°, covered, for 1½ hours.
Stir once half way through.

Notes

Chinese Stroganoff

You make this yummy dish a day ahead!

1½ lbs. beef cut for stroganoff
⅛ cup salad oil
1 red Bermuda onion, chopped
½ cup green onions, sliced thin
1 can (8 oz.) bamboo shoots, drained
1 can (8½ oz.) water chestnuts, drained and
    sliced
4 oz. mushrooms, sliced
½ cup beef broth (make from cubes)
1 Tablespoon sugar
2 Tablespoons cornstarch
½ cup soy sauce
1 can (1 lb.) sliced freestone peaches un-
    drained

Brown meat in oil.
Add onions (both kinds), bamboo shoots,
    water chestnuts, mushrooms,
    broth and sugar. Cover and simmer
    5 minutes.
Blend cornstarch with one Tablespoon water
    and the soy sauce. Add to mixture
    and simmer (stirring occasionally so
    it doesn't stick) until juice thickens.
Put in baking dish and refrigerate.
When ready to bake, pour peach juice over all,
    decorate with peaches, cover, and bake
    at 300 for 45 minutes or til hot through.

Serves 5

9

Notes

Chicken

And it's Tasty!

1/3 cup flour
   salt and pepper
4 chicken breasts
1/2 cup salad oil
1 yellow onion, chopped
1 clove garlic, minced
1 can (6 oz.) tomato paste
3/4 cup white wine
1 can (4 oz.) mushrooms and juice
1 tablespoon chopped parsley

Put flour, salt and pepper in paper bag
   and shake chicken in this, one
   piece at a time.
Heat salad oil and brown chicken.
   Remove chicken and put in one
   layer in baking dish. (I use 8" x 8")
Simmer garlic and onion in oil until
   onion is glossy.
Add tomato paste, wine, and mushrooms.
   Stir all and bring to a boil. Pour
   over chicken and refrigerate.
When ready, sprinkle with parsley and
   bake, covered (can use foil) for
   1 1/4 hours at 350°.

Serves 4   10

Notes

Top of the Stove Lamb Stew

A delicious winter meal!

1 clove garlic, minced
⅓ cup salad oil
1⅓ lbs lamb stew meat
   flour, salt, pepper
1 cup white wine
½ cup vermouth
1 cup water
4 carrots, peeled and cut in chunks
2 large turnips (cut in half) or 4 small
      turnips, peeled
2 yellow onions, peeled and halved
2 potatoes, peeled and cut in half
1 box (3½ oz.) fresh mushrooms, sliced.

Lightly brown garlic in oil.
Shake lamb in bag containing flour, salt
      and pepper. Brown in the oil with
      garlic.
Cool (so it won't spatter) and add wines
      and water. Cover and simmer
      one hour, stirring occasionally.
Meanwhile prepare vegetables and put in
      plastic bag in refrigerator. Put
      potatoes in dish of cold water
      so they won't turn dark.

Cont'd.   11

Notes

Top of the Stove Lamb Stew (cont'd.)

Refrigerate stew after simmering.

When ready, add vegetables (except mushrooms) and simmer, covered, for 40 minutes, adding mushrooms the last 10 minutes.

If, at any time you think you need more liquid, add wine.

Dinner for 4 —

Notes

Cays Firehouse Special

The men at the firehouse have great fun cooking — and they like it hot!

1½ lbs lean ground beef
1½ yellow onions, chopped
1 Tablespoon salad oil — or more
1 can (15 oz.) kidney beans, undrained
1 can (1 lb.) solid pack tomatoes, well drained
3 oz. bottled taco sauce
3 Tablespoons chili powder
1 can (4½ oz.) sliced olives, drained
1 pkg. (4 oz.) shredded cheddar cheese
1 medium pkg. corn chips
   shredded lettuce
2 cups commercial sour cream

In large frying pan brown beef and onions in
   oil. Drain well.
Add beans, tomatoes, taco sauce, chili powder
   and olives. Stir gently and simmer
   for about 15 minutes, uncovered.
In the bottom of a 3 QT. baking dish, put
   half the meat mixture. Sprinkle with
   half the cheese. Cover with corn chips.
   Repeat — however, if baking later, omit
   top layer of chips when refrigerating.
When ready to bake, place in 350° oven,
   covered, for 45 minutes. (Remember
   your top layer of chips if necessary.)
Let stand 5 minutes out of oven. Top with
   layer of lettuce and lastly a layer
   of sour cream — serve!

Serves 6 —

13

Notes

Luncheon Dish
For The ladies!

2 cups diced cooked chicken or Turkey
2 cans (4½ oz. each) chopped ripe olives
1 can (8 oz.) mushrooms, drained
¼ cup chopped onion
½ cup real mayonnaise
1 can (10¾ oz.) cream of chicken soup, undiluted
1 cup commercial sour cream
6 slices white bread (regular, not the
Thin sliced)

Trim crusts from bread and cut into
½" cubes.

Mix all and put in shallow greased
baking dish (I use 7½" x 12")
Refrigerate.

when ready, cover with foil and
bake at 300° for one hour.

Serves 8 —

14

Notes

Fish

You Try This one — I'm scared To!

Wrap whole, cleaned fish securely
   in foil.

Put fish in your dishwasher — no
   soap, please!

Run dishwasher Through iTs full
   cycle.

They say your fish will be
   perfectly cooked!

A good friend Tells me This
   reminds her of The old one
   about cooking your poT
   roasT Tied To The manifold
   beTween SF and Tahoe!

15

Notes

Stuffed Pimientos
A tasty, colorful side dish!

1 pkg. (3 oz.) cream cheese
1 pkg. (4 oz.) shredded cheddar cheese
2/3 cup dry seasoned poultry stuffing –
     crushed with rolling pin – measure
     after crushing.

2 eggs, beaten
1 heaping teaspoon wet mustard
1/2 teaspoon salt
1/4 teaspoon pepper
1/4 teaspoon Tabasco
2 cans (4 oz. each) whole pimientos

Whip cream cheese with a fork
     until smooth.
Add all but pimientos and mix well
Drain pimientos and stuff with
     this filling.
Grease a flat baking dish (I use
     6 1/2" x 10 1/2") and lay pimientos
     side by side.
Cover with sauce on following page.

16

Notes

Sauce for Pimientos

See preceding page

1/4 lb. fresh mushrooms
1 can (10 3/4 oz.) cream of celery soup
1 can (10 3/4 oz.) cream of mushroom soup
5 strips bacon

Chop mushrooms very fine.

Mix soup (undiluted) together and stir
    in mushrooms. Pour over
    pimientos. Refrigerate.

Fry bacon until crisp. Drain, crumble,
    and put in small covered jar.

When ready, sprinkle bacon over
    pimientos and bake, uncovered,
    at 350° for 45 minutes.

There is plenty of filling for 8 pimientos,
but sometimes there are 3 and sometimes 4 pimientos in one can. So if
you plan to serve 8, bear this in mind.

Notes

Stuffed Baked Potatoes

Great to keep on hand in the freezer!

4 baking potatoes
2 Tablespoons margarine, cut up
   milk — about 3 oz. more or less
1 egg, slightly beaten
1 pkg. (4 oz.) shredded cheddar cheese
2 Tablespoons chopped chives, fresh or
      freeze dried
salt and pepper to taste
paprika

Wash potatoes well — dry skins and rub
   them lightly with margarine or
   bacon grease. Bake at 425° for
   one hour.
Cut in half lengthwise with sharp butcher
   knife. Scoop out insides carefully
   and put in large mixing bowl.
Add the 2 Tablespoons margarine, milk,
   egg, and beat with electric beater
   until smooth — no lumps!
Add cheese, chives, salt and pepper. Mix well.
Heap back in shells. Put on cookie sheet.
Sprinkle with paprika. Freeze thoroughly
      Put in plastic bag.
When ready, thaw, and bake at 350°
   for 25 minutes.

Serves 8

18

Notes

Party Salad for Ten

To me, This recipe alone is worth
The cost of the book!

½ pkg. (10 oz. pkg.) fresh spinach, Torn in pieces
    salt and pepper To Taste — ½ Teaspoon sugar
6 hardboiled eggs, finely chopped
½ lb. julienne boiled ham (I use The cello pkgs.
    of sandwich ham and slice Thin)
1 small or ½ large head iceberg lettuce, Torn
    or shredded
    salt and pepper To Taste — ½ Teaspoon sugar
1 pkg. (10 oz.) frozen peas, Thawed but not
    cooked
1 red Bermuda onion, peeled and Thinly
    sliced
1 cup commercial sour cream
1 pint real mayonnaise
½ lb. julienne Swiss cheese
½ lb. bacon, crisply cooked and crumbled

IT is important To drain everyThing well.

In The bottom of a large glass or wooden
    salad bowl, spread The spinach.
    Sprinkle with salt, pepper and sugar.
Add a layer of The eggs.

cont'd   19

Notes

20

Party Salad for Ten (cont'd.)

Add a layer of the ham.

Add a layer of lettuce and sprinkle with
salt, pepper and sugar.

Scatter peas over all.

Pull onion slices into rings and
spread on salad.

Mix sour cream and mayonnaise
and spread evenly all over top.

Arrange cheese over all.

Cover bowl with plastic wrap and
refrigerate overnight.

Just before serving, sprinkle with
bacon.

Do <u>not</u> toss. Serve portions all
the way to the bottom of
the bowl.

For a main course salad meal,
you can substitute tuna, crab,
shrimp or lobster for the
bacon.

Notes

Diet Soup

We love this!

1 can (10¾ oz.) cream of chicken soup
¼ cup juice from canned mushrooms
1 cup nonfat milk
½ cup water
½ teaspoon curry powder
1 Tablespoon green onion Tops

Heat all slowly, stirring until
smooth.

Or make ahead, refrigerate, and
reheat later.

Makes 3 8-oz. servings ⸺

21

Notes

Vegetable Mold

One of my favorite party molds!

1 1/4 cup celery, chopped
1 yellow onion, chopped
1/2 large green pepper, chopped. (First remove
    seeds and membranes inside.)
1 cucumber, chopped. (Remove Tips but don't peel.)
1 pkg. (8 oz.) cream cheese, softened
1 can (10 3/4 oz.) tomato soup, undiluted
1/4 cup lemon juice
3/4 cup water
2 pkgs. (3 oz each) lemon jello. Or one 6 oz. pkg.
1 cup real mayonnaise
1/2 cup chopped walnuts
    parsley for top

Put celery, onion, pepper and cucumber
    through food grinder using medium blade.
    Drain in colander or large strainer.
Whip cheese with fork, add soup, and mix well.
Bring lemon juice and water to a boil. Add
    jello and stir until dissolved.
Pour cheese-soup mixture into jello. Add
    vegetables and mayonnaise. Beat all
    with egg beater. Fold in nuts.
Grease a flat 2-qt. dish with salad oil and
    pour all into dish. Refrigerate overnight
    until firm.
Sprinkle with parsley; cut in squares to serve
    on lettuce. You can mix a little red wine
    vinegar with mayonnaise and put a dab
    on top each square.
Serves 10 easily.

22

Notes

Weekend Soups

Onion and Cheese:

    1 can or pkg. onion soup
    1 slice American cheese - per person
    1 slice French bread - per person

Make soup according to directions
In each bowl put one slice toasted bread,
    lightly buttered.
Top the toast with a slice of cheese.
Over all this pour the hot soup.

Corn:

    1 can (17 oz.) cream style corn
    1 can (10½ oz.) chicken and rice soup
    1 pint Half and Half
    salt to taste
    paprika

Whir soups in blender.
Add Half and Half, salt, and heat slowly,
    stirring often. Do not boil.
Sprinkle paprika on each bowl before serving.

Mystery Soup: (You can't guess contents!)

    1 can (10½ oz.) cream of Asparagus soup, undiluted
    1 cup milk (nonfat is OK)
    ¼ Teaspoon Tabasco - ½ Teaspoon celery salt
    1 cup commercial sour cream
    1 Thin slice of onion, minced
        minced chives

Mix all but chives in blender. Refrigerate.
Reheat, stirring, and serve in mugs with
    chives on top.

23

Notes

Lazey-Dazey Cake

A favorite of young and old alike!

1 pkg. (18½ oz.) lemon cake mix
1 pkg. (3½ oz.) instant vanilla pudding
¾ cup real mayonnaise
¾ cup water
4 whole eggs
    powdered sugar

Preheat oven to 350° and line a
    7½" X 12" X 2" baking dish with
    brown paper
Put first four ingredients in large
    mixing bowl and mix with
    electric beater at low speed
    until smooth.
Add eggs, one at a time, beating a
    minimum of one minute at
    medium speed after each addition.
Pour batter into lined dish and bake at
    350° for 50 minutes. Cool in dish
    for 15 minutes and remove.
When completely cool, sift sugar on top
    or serve "as is" with fresh fruit.
If you freeze it, thaw before adding sugar.
Try different flavors of cake and pudding mixes.

Right size dish is important.

24

Notes

Canton Dessert
But it's not Chinese!

4 cups apples, peeled, cored, and chopped fine
   (takes about 5 or 6 apples)

2 cups sugar
2 eggs, beaten
½ cup salad oil
2 teaspoons vanilla
2 cups flour
2 teaspoons baking soda (not powder).
2 teaspoons cinnamon
1 teaspoon salt
1 cup chopped walnuts

Mix apples with sugar and set aside while
   you do the rest.
Mix eggs and salad oil together and beat
   a bit. Add vanilla to this.
Sift together the dry ingredients.
Now add the egg mixture to apple-sugar
   and mix well.
Next add the dry ingredients, mixing well.
Fold in nuts.
Put all in greased, floured 9" x 13" flat baking
   dish and bake at 325° for 35-40 minutes.
Serve warm ~ or cool in dish. It's great plain,
   topped with whipped cream, vanilla ice
   cream, or hard sauce. Freezes well.

25

Notes

Favorite Bars
And they freeze beautifully!

3 cups flour
2 1/2 teaspoons baking powder
1/2 teaspoon salt
2 1/4 cups dark brown sugar
2/3 cup butter or margarine, melted
4 eggs, beaten
1 large pkg. (12 oz.) chocolate bits
2 teaspoons vanilla

Sift together the flour, baking powder, and salt.

Add sugar to melted shortening, creaming well!

Add eggs, flour mixture, bits and vanilla, creaming well after each addition.

Spread in 9" x 13" greased pan or baking dish. (You must use this size!)

Bake at 350° for 25 minutes. They should come out light brown and not overcooked. Cool in pan out of oven before cutting.

Makes 50-60 bars about 1 1/4" x 1 1/4".

Notes

Unusual Appetizer

I hope you like sprouts!

1 pkg. (10 oz.) frozen Brussels sprouts
½ cup juice from a bottle of dill pickles

Thaw sprouts and cook minimum
amount of Time. Drain.

Put in a flat dish - I use a loaf
baking dish - and pour The
pickle juice over Them. Put
in refrigerator overnight.
The next morning spoon The juice
over them again.

when ready To serve, drain, and
serve with Toothpicks.

The friend who gave me This said,
Those who claim They dislike sprouts
eat the most!

Notes

Ready Breakfast
Really provides variety!

When ground round is specially priced,
   buy several pounds and make
   into patties.
Cover a cookie sheet with foil and
   put patties - almost touching - on
   sheet. Put in freezer.
When thoroughly frozen, remove patties
   from cookie sheet and put in
   plastic bag. Return to freezer.
You can fry these frozen (takes a
   little longer) or take desired
   number from freezer and put
   in refrigerator the night before
   you want to use them.
Great for breakfast ~ and the kids
   do love a handy hamburger
   for lunch or after school.
You can do the same with pork sausage
   from your butcher - not previously
   frozen.
Buy slices of cooked ham, cut in serving
   sizes and follow same method.
   Also steak.

28

Notes

Marinade for Beef

And, in particular, This is absolutely
marvelous for London Broil!

1/2 cup salad oil
1/2 cup soy sauce
1/2 cup red wine
1 Tablespoon lemon juice
2 cloves garlic, finely minced
1/4 Teaspoon pepper
1/4 Teaspoon salt
1 Teaspoon monosodium glutamate (MSG)
1 Tablespoon sugar

Mix all Together and beat with egg beater.
Marinate meat overnight, Turning
occasionally — in refrigerator.

Notes

Marinade for Fish

Makes even a "so-so" fish taste great!

1 clove garlic, finely minced
½ cup soy sauce
½ cup red wine
    juice of half a large lemon
    minced green onion (see below)

Make 2 or 3 slant-wise gashes in
    each side of fish.
Marinate several hours, turning once.
Sprinkle with green onion before
    baking but not before broiling or
    onion will burn.

This marinade is the right amount
    for 2 fish the size of an average
    Rockfish. Use a "flattish" dish.

Notes

Christmas Breakfast

You make it the day before, and it bakes happily while you open your gifts Xmas morning!

7 slices white bread (regular, not thin sliced)
2 pkgs. (4 oz. each) shredded cheddar cheese
6 eggs
3 cups milk
1/2 teaspoon salt
1/4 teaspoon pepper
1 teaspoon dry mustard
3 strips bacon, cut in half

Trim crusts from bread. Crumble bread.
Mix bread and cheese and spread in bottom
    of greased 7 1/2" x 12" flat baking dish.
Beat eggs and milk together and stir in
    the salt, pepper, and mustard. Pour
    this over bread-cheese.
Lay bacon on top.
Refrigerate overnight.
The next morning bake, uncovered, at
    350° for 50 to 55 minutes.

Remove from oven just after guests sit down.
Otherwise, it may tend to sink — tastes just as
great — but doesn't look as glamorous.

Serves 6 —

Notes

Virginia Sausage

And This recipe really came from Virginia!

About 5 lbs. fresh pork, Picnic or Boston Butt
2 Tablespoons sage
1 Tablespoon salt
1 Teaspoon ground red pepper
1 Teaspoon black pepper

Cut away the bone, skin and all excess fat. Cut meat into 1" cubes.

Blend together all the seasonings.

Mix meat well with seasonings, using your hands. Let stand in refrigerator overnight.

The next day put the meat through the food grinder twice, first using the coarse plate, then the medium. (If you don't have a medium, use coarse twice.) Grind slowly to prevent meat from overheating.

cont'd

Notes

Virginia Sausage
Cont'd

Make into patties of desired size.
Wrap patties individually in
plastic wrap and freeze. Or
put on cookie sheets, freeze,
put in a plastic bag and
pop back into freezer. I remove
desired amount of patties from
freezer and put them in the
refrigerator the night before
I plan to use them.

For best flavor you should consume
this within six weeks.

Cook patties slowly until brown.
Fresh pork should always
be well done, but do not
overcook.

If you want to try different amounts,
a good mixture for sausage is:
2/3 lean and 1/3 fat — but
we prefer it lean. You should
also adjust your seasonings
to your preference.

Notes

Special Tea

A favorite with the college group!

1 large jar TANG (18 oz.)
½ cup instant Tea
1½ cups sugar
1 Teaspoon ground cinnamon
½ Teaspoon ground cloves
    lemon slices

Mix Together all but lemon and keep
    in closed jar.
For each cup of boiling water, use 2 or
    3 heaping Teaspoons of mixture.
Add Thin slice of lemon To each cup
    of hot Tea.

Notes

Note

One half the author's profit from all six "Make it Now" books is given to:

The Cystic Fibrosis Foundation
6000 Executive Blvd.
Suite 309
Rockville, Md. 20852

If you would like a copy of any of the other "Make it Now" books, ask your local gift or bookstore or write for information to:

Barbara Goodfellow
409 First Street
Coronado, Calif. 92118

Notes

Notes

Notes

Notes

Notes